EACHWHAT

VOLUME 1

a collection of poem brut (ish)

the gestural, the instinctual, the scribbled and the scrawled

PAUL HAWKINS

/

BOB MODEM

KFS

Newton-le-Willows

Published in the United Kingdom in 2020
by The Knives Forks And Spoons Press,
51 Pipit Avenue,
Newton-le-Willows,
Merseyside,
WA12 9RG.

ISBN 978-1-912211-67-8

Acknowledgements:

Lots of love to: my partner-in-crime Sarer Scotthorne; Second Step, Bristol; Steve Fowler; Alec Newman; Steve Ryan; & to everyone involved in the Poem Brut project, who have all directly or indirectly helped make *EACHWHAT: Vol. 1* happen. Thank you.

Some of the artworks in *EACHWHAT Vol. 1* have appeared in the following; *The Arsonist* (Burning House Press, 2017), *Felt - Aesthetics of Grey* (Zeno Press, 2018), *FAKE* (Corrupted Poetry, 2020), *Tenebrae IV: Pomes & Joys for Anna Mendelssohn* (Fathomsun Press, 2020), *Empty Mirror, and 3:AM magazine*. With thanks to all the editors.

Some of these artworks have been part of the following group exhibitions; HESTERGLOCK at the Neck of the Woods Community Cafe, Bristol (2020), AN INVISIBLE POETRY: THE POET'S BRUT at The Poetry Café, London (2019), POTOS: explorations in handwritten poetry & analog photography at The Museum of Futures (2019), INSTAPOETRY at The National Poetry Library, London (2018), POEM BRUT AT SPIKE ISLAND at Spike Island, Bristol (2018)and HARD TO READ POEM BRUT at Rich Mix Gallery, London (2018). Many thanks to everyone involved in making these events happen.

LOTTERY FUNDED
Supported using public funding by
ARTS COUNCIL ENGLAND

for Sarer

CONTENTS

frag

G R E Y (for anna mendelssohn)

toriot

Frag

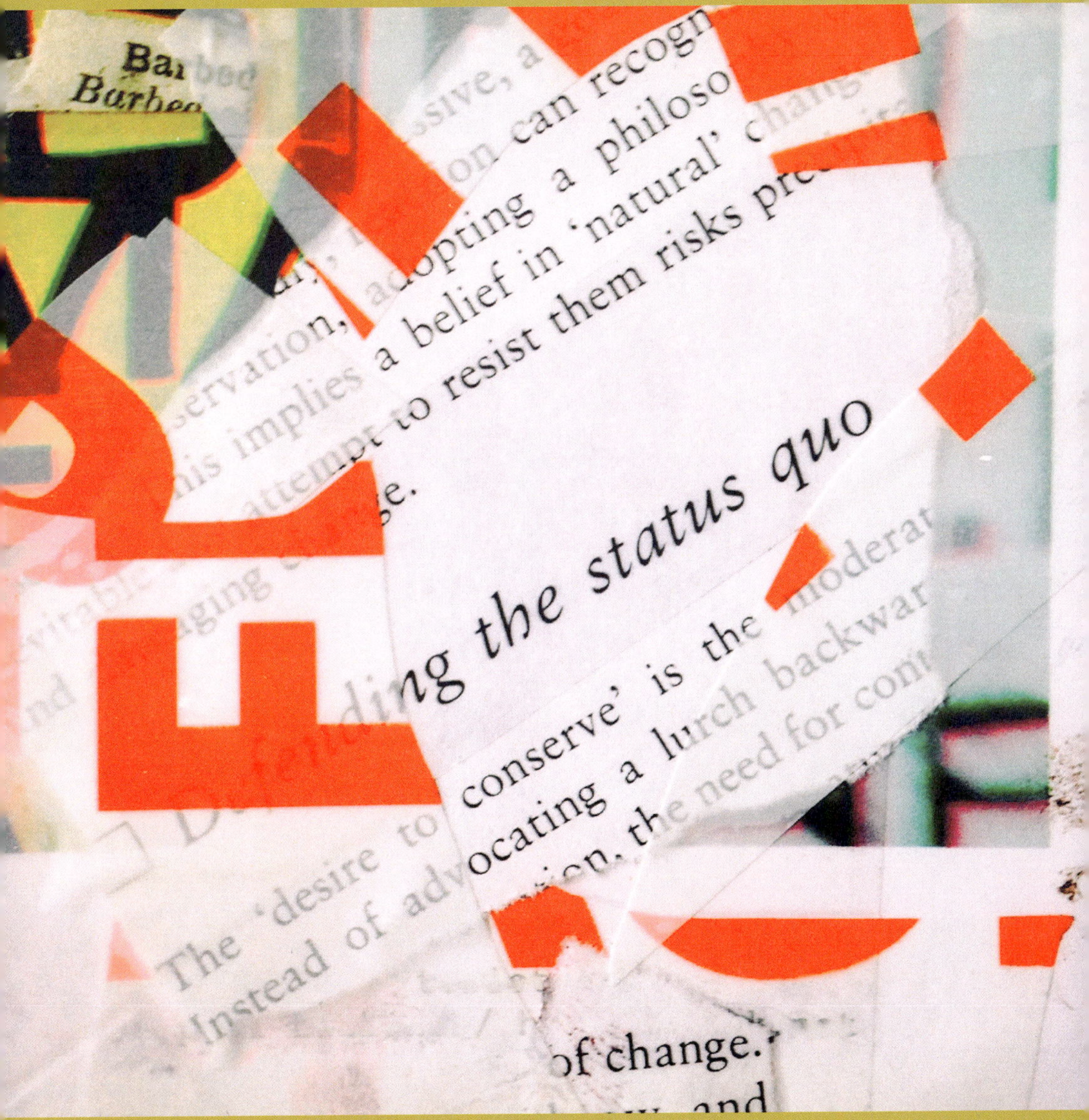
on can recogn
adopting a philoso
a belief in 'natural' chang
to resist them risks pre
servation,
his implies
Defending the status quo
conserve' is the moderat
ocating a lurch backwar
the need for con
The 'desire to
Instead of adv
of change.

"Everything has
the trains keep

End-irons
be one's end. The cause or agent
death.
This apoplexie will be his end.
Shakespeare : 2 Henry IV, iv, 4.

GREY
(for Anna Mendelssohn)

gewitter rosen erhellt you gold
roomy eye young gynaecium
revolution easily you good ripple
ecstasy you guide ring ever you gogol
rush exquisite young **groovy**
raised eyebrows yes
greyed retired el york greco
ravanchol ever you glance rain eyes yet
gilding rusts expects you garibaldi
responsibility enterprise you guided
retribution earth yourself given reign
ends you good rides eliding young
glass red enamel yet gone revolution
elan your grains **reticent entrance**
you grouting route earth
yesterday green right easy
years germanically

good ripple
good ripple
ever you gogol
you gogol
groovy
groovy
yes
rows yes
york greco
greco
rain eyes yet

good ripple
ever you gogol
groovy
brows yes
york greco
rain eyes yet

good ripple
ripple
ever you gogol
you gogol
groovy
rows yes
greco
greco
eyes yet

racking
russian
reawakening
retina
expected
your grammar
you goodbye
yourself guernica
guernica reminiscent
expanse yellow green raised either
yet grasps reference economy years
raised either
exhibition economy years
emblematic yes
emblematic yes guilt
republican
relationship
you earnings
existence you
garibaldi
guided

gewitter rosen erhellt you gold
roomy eye young gynaecium
revolution easily you good ripple
ecstasy you guide ring ever you gogol
rush exquisite young groovy
raised eyebrows yes
greyed retired el york greco
ravanchol ever you glance rain eyes yet

racking escape you gangsters
russian [illegible] gangsters
reawaken [illegible] greened
retina [illegible] green
expected [illegible] renou
your [illegible] respect end
you good [illegible] echoes
yourself [illegible] evening
yourself [illegible] reminiscent
expanse yellow green raised either
yet grasp [illegible] raised either
guns [illegible] economy years
grundy [illegible] you
gown [illegible]
raw [illegible] gunt
equality [illegible] republican
every [illegible] relationship
you [illegible] earnings
grey [illegible] right existence you
gilding rusts expects you garibaldi
responsibility enterprise you guided
retribution earth yourself given reign
ends you good rides eliding young
glass red enamel yet gone revolution
elan your grains reticent entrance
you grouting route earth
yesterday green right easy
years germanically

you ga
you grea
rammar rel
oodbye. repe
guernica
guernica
e yellow green
asps reference e
removed exh
ndig right emble
room ephe
you gig

grammar relation **ECHOES** *you*

good
b y e
repeats
evening
yourself
guern

i e a
reminis
c e n t
expans
e
yellow
green
raised
either
y e t
grasp
s
referen
c e
econo
m y
years
guns
remove
d
exhibiti
on *you*
grun
d i g
right
emble
matic
y e s
gown
room
ephem

era yes
guilt
r a w
e a r
y o *u*
giggl
e
republi
c a n
equalit
y yes
greek
relation
s h i p
every
y o u
game
s really
earning
s you
groun
d s
right
existen
ce *you*
grey
ring
euro
p a
your
self
glass
r e d
expans
e

good
b y e
repeats
evening
yourself
guern

i c a
reminis
c e n t
expans
e
yellow
green
raised
either
y e t
grasp
s
referen
c e
econo
m y
y e a r s
g u n s
remove
d
exhibiti
on *you*
grun
d i g
right
emble
matic
y e s
gown
r o o m
ephem

era yes
guilt
r a w
e a r
y o *u*
giggl
e
republi
c a n
equalit
y yes
greek
relation
s h i p
e v e r y
y a *u*
game
s really
earning
s you
groun
d s
r i g h t
existen
ce *you*
grey
ring
euro
p a
your
s e l f
glass
r e d
expans
e

glass red enamel yet

gone revolution elan *you*r

grains **reticent entrance** *you*

grouting route earth yesterday

g r e e n r i g h t e a s y y e a r s

germanically reactions **end** *you***nger**

giggling racking escape *you*

gangsters russian everywhere *you*

greeted reawakenings exists *you*

green retina exist you

games renoir expected you

great respect end *you*r

grammar relation **ECHOES** *you*

goodbye repeats evening *you*rself

guernica reminiscent expanse yellow

green **raised either** yet

grasps reference economy years

guns removed exhibition *you*

grundig right emblematic yes

gown room ephemera yes

guilt raw **ear** *you*

giggle republican equality yes

greek relationship every *you*

games really earnings you

grounds right existence *you*

grey ring europa yourself

glass red expanse

gewitter rosen erhellt *you* gold
roomy eye *you*ng gynaecium
revolution easily *you* good ripple
ecstasy *you* guide ring ever *you* gogol
rush exquisite *you*ng **groovy**
raised eyebrows yes
greyed retired el york greco
ravanchol ever *you* glance rain eyes yet
gilding rusts expects *you* garibaldi
responsibility enterprise you guided
retribution earth *you*rself given reign
ends *you* good rides eliding *you*ng

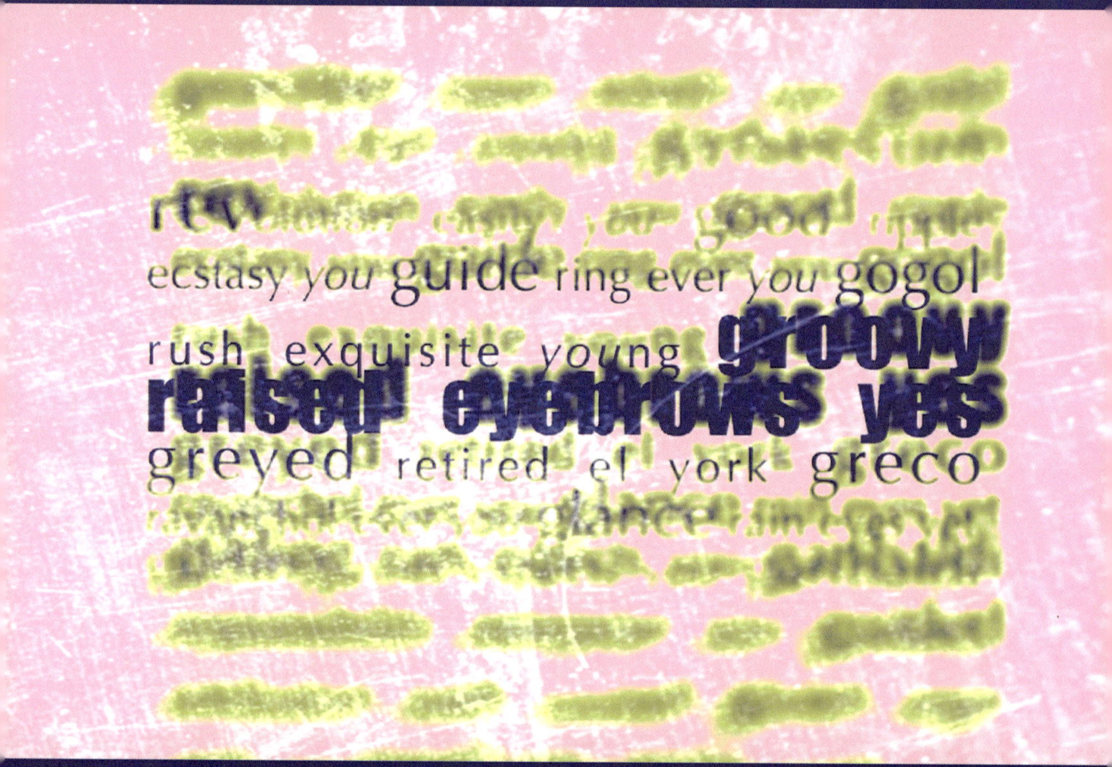
ecstasy you guide ring ever you gogol
rush exquisite young groovy
raised eyebrows yes
greyed retired el york greco

~~glass red enamel yet gone revolution~~
~~elan *your* grains reticent entrance~~
~~*you* grouting route earth~~
~~yesterday green right easy years~~
~~germanically reactions end *youn*ger~~
~~giggling racking escape *you*~~
~~gangsters russian everywhere *you*~~
~~greeted reawakenings exists *you*~~
~~green retina exist you **games** renoir~~
~~expected you great respect end *your*~~
~~grammar relation~~ ECHOES ~~*you*~~

toriot

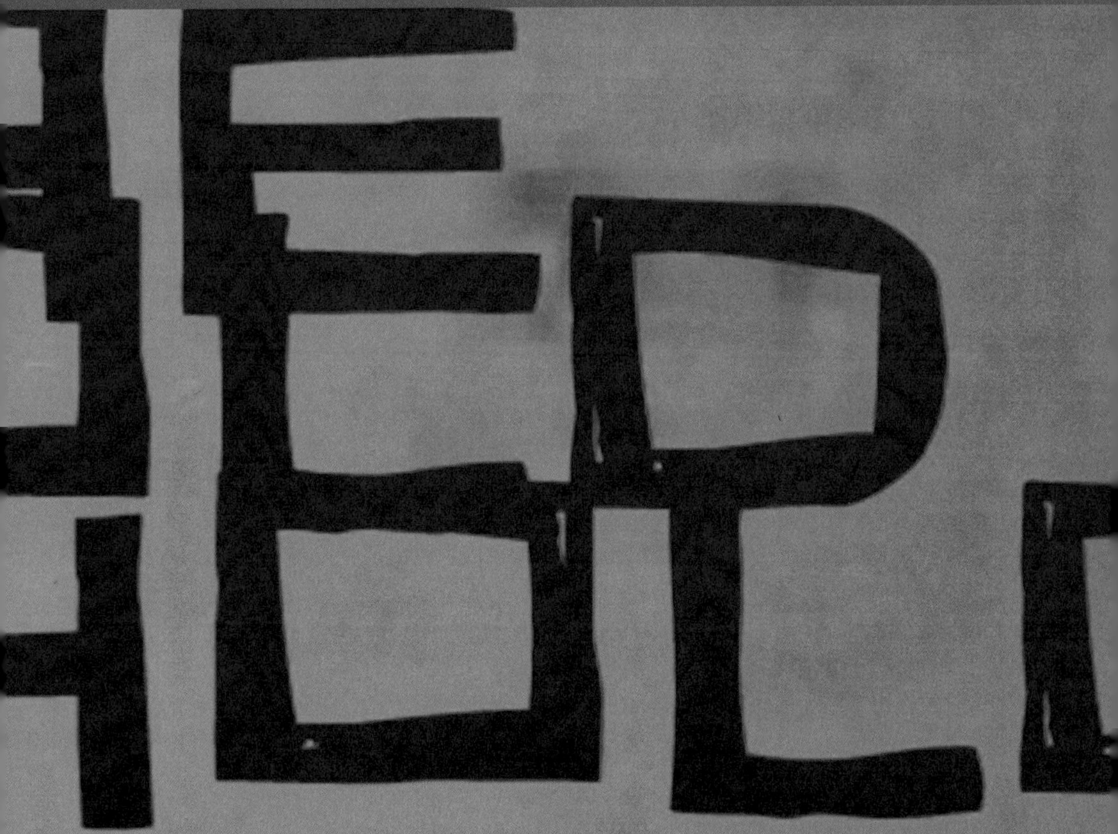

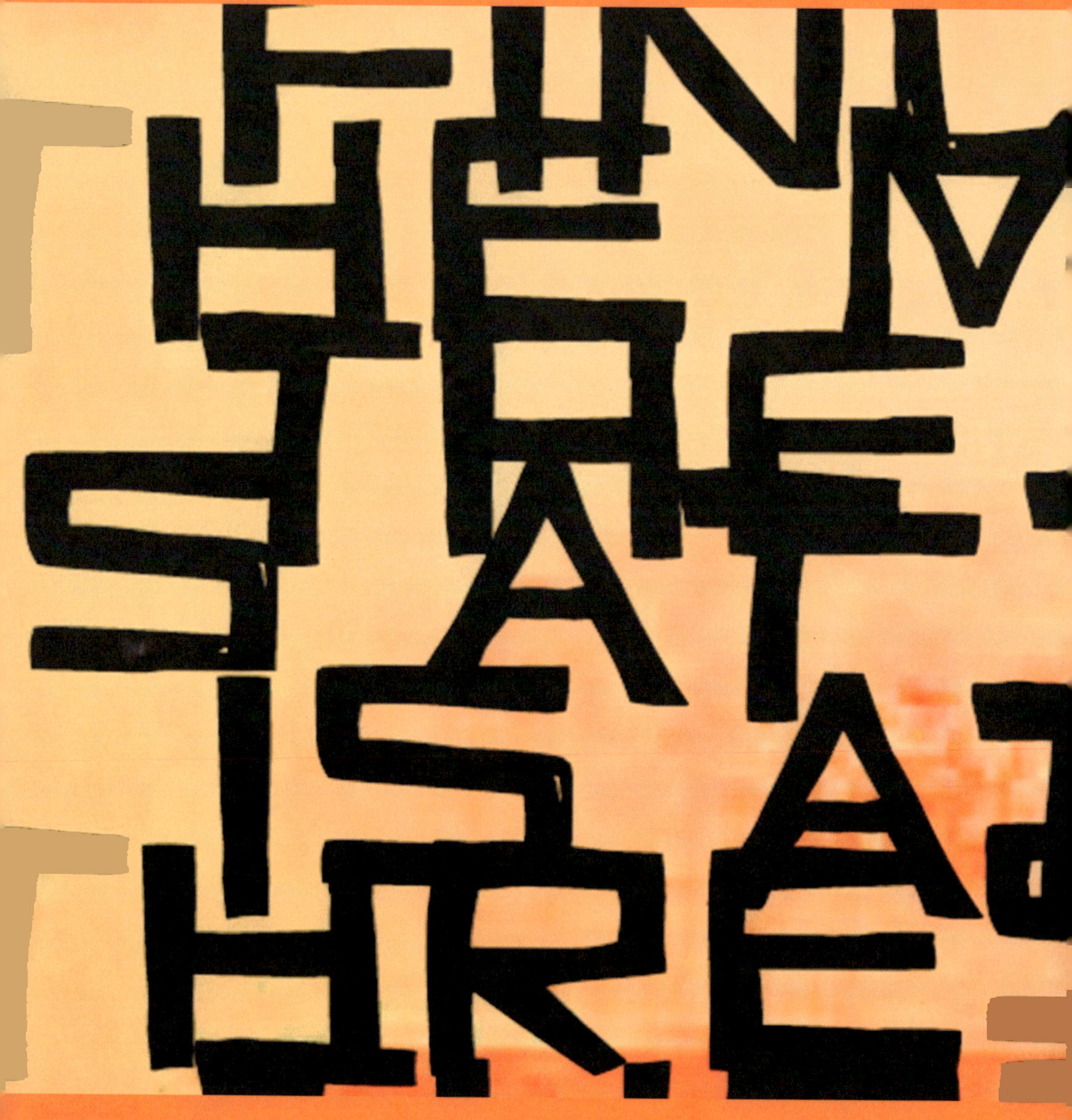

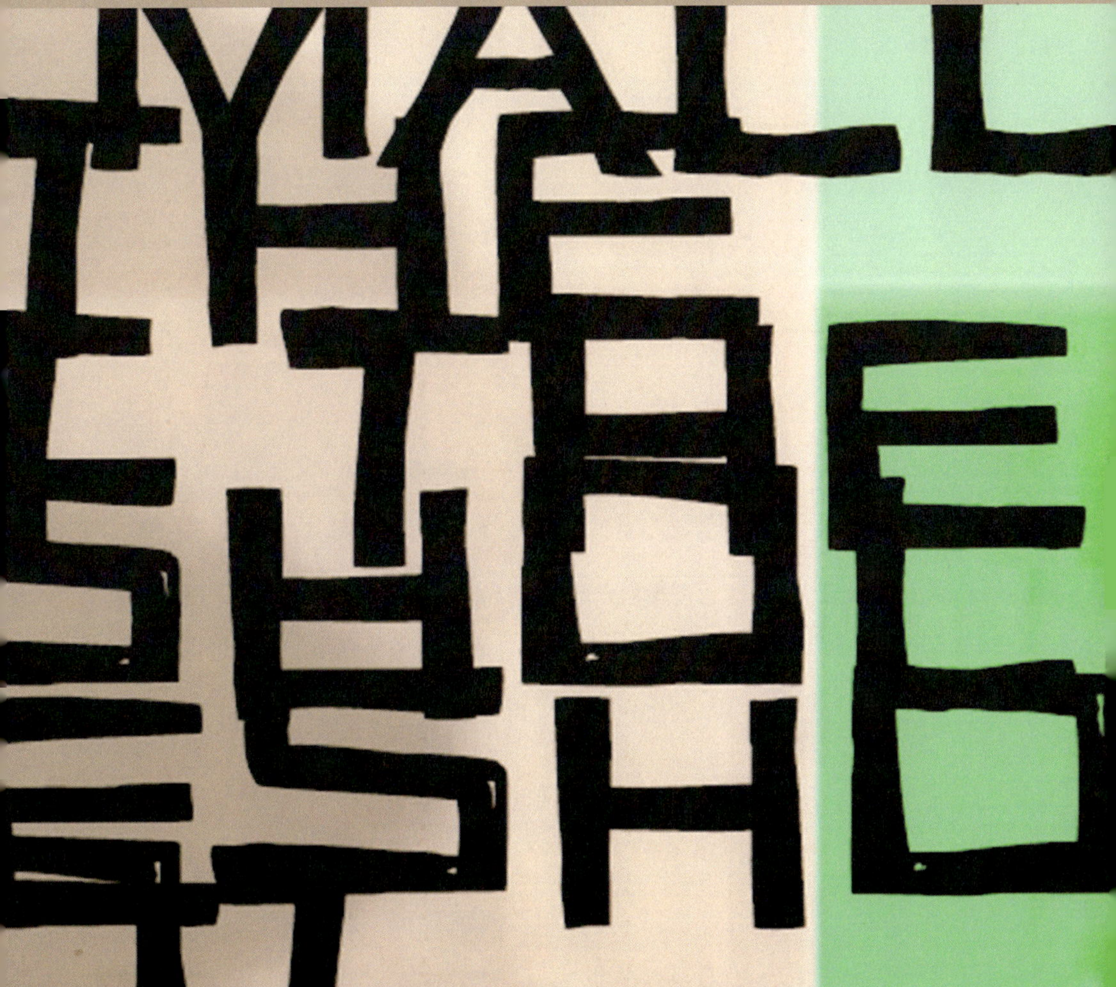

ALL

ENTS
UT
ALL

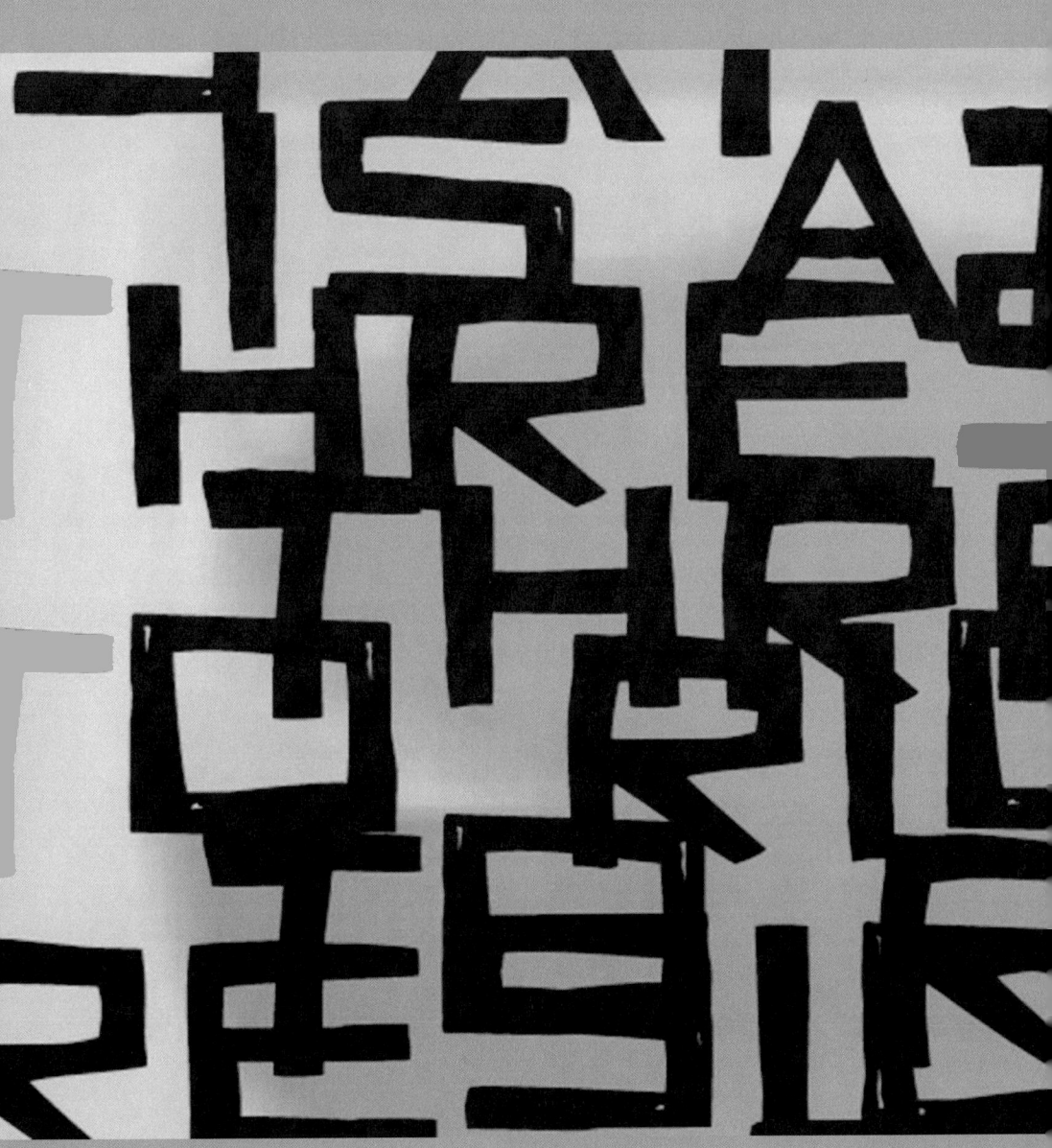

FIND

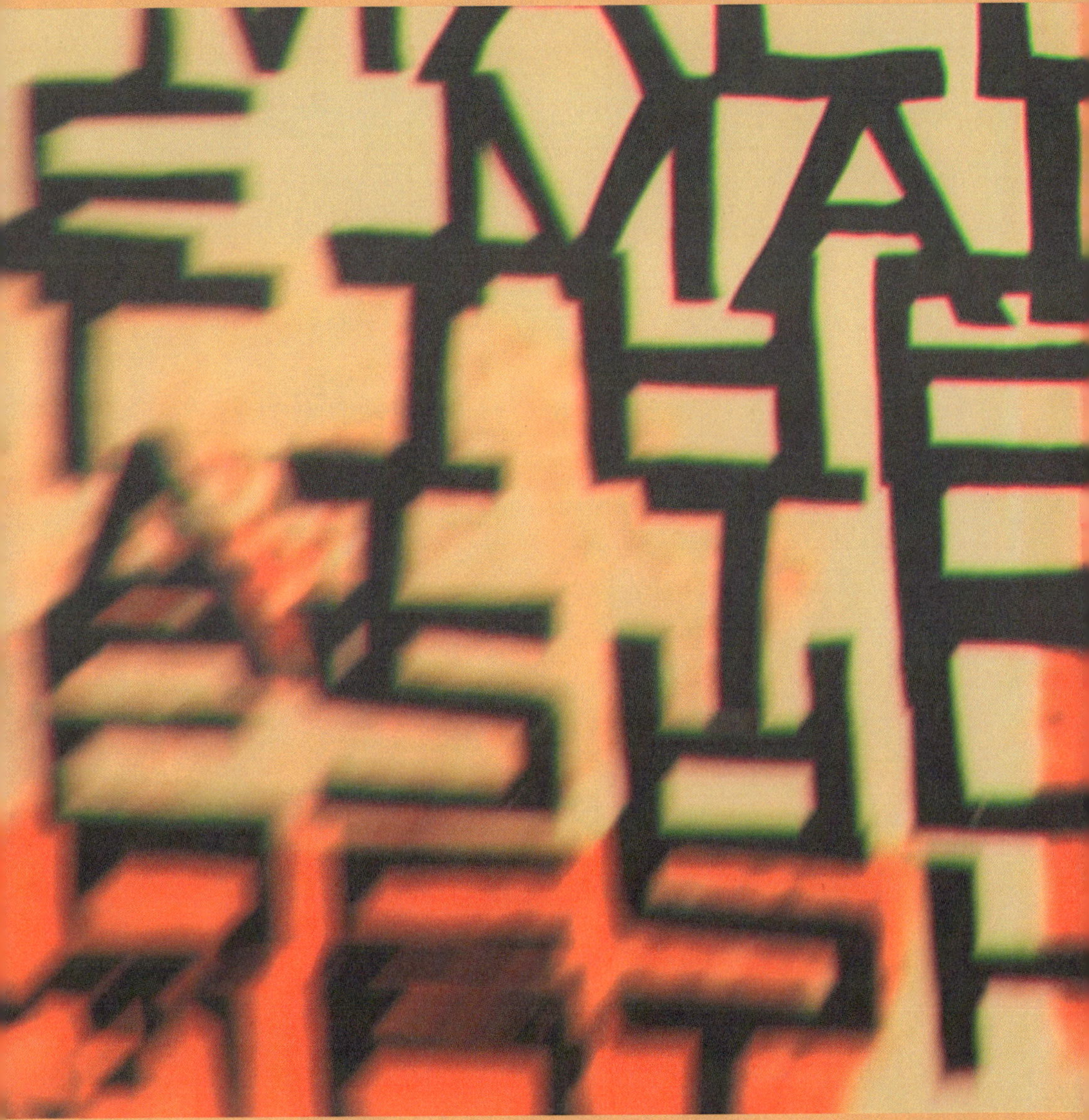

A Word on Poem Brut

"How vain is it to think that words can penetrate the mystery of our being. Rightly used they may make evident our ignorance of ourselves, and this is much."

– P.B. Shelley

Becoming involved with a project (school of, movement, whatever) called Poem Brut has had an exciting and profoundly positive effect on developing new ideas about how, what, and why I make things. Poem Brut takes it's cue(s) from the COBRA movement, whose main focuses were: abstract art; the use of vibrant, brilliant colour, fierce brushwork and contorted human figures – often inspired by naive, primitive folk art, non-western tribal art; the creative art of children and outsider art (with an emphasis on neurodivergence); experimentation with materials, methods and forms were also essential, radical elements.

Poem Brut is an exploration of artistic creative writing (poetry and colour, handwriting, composition, abstraction, scribbling, illustration), a project that affirms the possibilities of the page, the pen, the pencil in a computer age. It's curated by SJ Fowler, and has, to date, generated over a dozen live events; nearly 100 commissions; exhibitions at The Museum of Futures, The Poetry Society and Rich Mix; and a series of brand new books. Poem Brut has offered an alternative understanding of 21st century literature, collaboration and performance since 2017.

Personally, I'd been feeling a growing dis-ease with the more mainstream, traditional forms of an overtly *Parnissian Poetry*, to the extent that *unlearning* these ancient rules became all-important to me. In *All Religions Are One*, William Blake complained that he couldn't express himself in verse: "No man can think write or speak from his heart, but he must intend truth. Thus all sects of Philosophy are from the Poetic Genius, adapted to the weaknesses of every individual." Furthermore, *Blake's Doors of Perception* was an opening up, a personal revelation. Poem Brut was beginning to open doors of expression for me.

I've been fortunate to be involved with Poem Brut, either as a performer, an artist, an audience member, as a collaborator or as a publisher, since 2017. This new *Poem Brut-ish approach* gradually developed (and is still developing) through engaging with poets/artists/performers, such as: Khaled Hakim, Jacqueline Ennis Cole, Julia Rose Lewis, Mischa Foster Poole, Saradha Soobrayen, Patrick Cosgrove, Sarah Dawson, Michael Sutton, Stephen Emmerson, Martin Wakefield, Iris Colomb, James Caley (and many, many more). It began to feel right, exciting, inspiring, supportive. It became a rich site of collaboration and imagination. I stopped following so rigorously what I had learn't and felt a sense of satisfaction. Of coherency. And that's important to me.

I admit to having to regularly remind myself that poetry, artistic creative writing, Poem Brut etc. should not be taken too seriously and certainly by itself is never going to change the world for the better. Let's not kid ourselves. And it isn't the only or even the main way I attempt to communicate how understand the world. Far from it. But it does play an important role, like a pressure-valve does. I'm no stranger to the mental health industry: I have a diagnosis of Borderline Personality Disorder, which impacts hugely on how I understand the world, how I engage with it, how I operate within it and with other humans, other structures. So it follows that it impacts on how I make art in the chaos of the 21st century. I tried to put this into words in the introduction to a book I wrote called *Place Waste Dissent* around 5 years ago, that this re-calibrating, this re-wiring is ongoing, it's a *work-in-progress ... (that) there is, in the main, discordance, with moments of incredible excitement, possibility and beauty; a negotiated, collaborative, experimental serenity (however momen-tary).*

The next collection of this work-in-progress is this book: *EACHWHAT Vol. 2: A Poem Brut-ish culmination of the gestural, the instinctual, the scribbled and the scrawled over the past few years.* I'm confident that *EACHWHAT Vol. 1* won't be widely read, but don't let that stop you. I'm proud of it. *EACHWHAT Vol. 2* follows in 2021.

More info: www.poembrut.com.

– Paul H / Bob M

About the Author

Paul Hawkins (aka Bob Modem) works mainly in poetry, visual art & performance. He has co-run & been co-editor at Hesterglock Press since 2013. They have written a number of books of poetry (some collaborative, some not) including *Contumacy* (Erbacce Press 2014), *Servant Drone*, with Bruno Neiva (KFS Press 2015), *Place Waste Dissent* (Influx Press 2015), *the 50//fifty*, with Michael Harford (Hesterglock Press 2018), *Lou Ham: Racing Anthropocene Statments* (Dostoyevsky Wannabe 2018), *Go Sift Omen* (KFS Press 2019) & others. Their work has been performed widely throughout Europe and exhibited in London, Sheffield, Bournemouth & Bristol. They curated *Diisonance*, a series of collaborative artworks with artist Steve Ryan, which featured exhibitions, performances & an anthology, and co-edited the dubwise, collaborative visual art/poetry athology, *Original Plus Dub* (Hesterglock Press, 2019). *EACHWHAT Vol. 1* is their first collection of Poem Brut-ish visual art & collage. *EACHWHAT Vol. 2* will follow in 2021.

All information is at eachwhat.com & hesterglock.net.

www.ingramcontent.com/pod-product-compliance
Lightning Source LLC
Chambersburg PA
CBRC102059150426
43193CB00007B/64

* 9 7 8 1 9 1 2 2 1 1 6 7 8 *